Beyond the Gate

Also by Clare Best

Poetry
Treasure Ground, HappenStance 2009
Excisions, Waterloo Press 2011
Breastless, Pighog Press 2011
Each Other, Waterloo Press 2019
End of Season, Coast to Coast to Coast 2020

Collaborative works
CELL (with Michaela Ridgway and Katy Mawhood), Frogmore
  Press 2015
Springlines (with Mary Anne Aytoun-Ellis), Little Toller Books 2017
End of Season / Fine di stagione (with Franca Mancinelli, John
  Taylor, Katy Mawhood), Frogmore Press 2022

Memoir
The Missing List, Linen Press 2018

Works for stage and platform
Vacant Possession (with Sara Clifford) – site specific theatre,
  Lewes 2015
The Apothecary (with composer Amy Crankshaw) – chamber
  opera, London 2020
Rotten Kid (with composer Erchao Gu) – chamber opera,
  London 2021
TEXT (with composer Michael Bascom) – chamber opera,
  London 2021
Three Songs from Springlines (with composer Hugh Morris) –
  songs, Ludlow 2021
End of Season (with composer Amy Crankshaw) – song cycle,
  Italy 2022

Online
Breastless: Encounters with risk-reducing surgery – multimedia
  project with photography by Laura Stevens at
  https://reframe.sussex.ac.uk/lifewritingprojects/
  body/breastless-encounters-with-risk-reducing-
  surgery-by-clare-best

BEYOND THE GATE

CLARE BEST

First published in 2023 by
Worple Press
www.worplepress.co.uk

Printed by imprintdigital
Upton Pyne, Exeter
www.digital.imprint.co.uk

Typesetting and cover design by The Book Typesetters
hello@thebooktypesetters.com
07422 598 168
www.thebooktypesetters.com

ISBN 978-1-905208-50-0

Acknowledgements

My thanks to the editors of the following publications, where earlier versions of some of the poems in *Beyond the Gate* have appeared: *Allegro*, *Black Nore Review*, *Confluence*, *Envoi*, *Finished Creatures*, *14 Magazine*, *Ink Sweat & Tears*, *Magma*, *Poetry and Covid*, *Tabula Rasa* (Linen Press 2023), *The Friday Poem*, *The Frogmore Papers*, *The Stony Thursday Book*, *Watermarks* (Frogmore Press 2017).

A number of the poems written for the *Springlines* project are included here: 'Lark walk, February', 'Book of water', 'Dewpond', 'Cart pond', 'In Markstakes Wood', 'The pools at Glyndebourne' and 'Water spirit' were all exhibited in *Springlines* exhibitions between 2015 and 2018 at Glyndebourne, at Tunbridge Wells Museum & Art Gallery and at St Barbe Museum & Art Gallery and all were published in *Springlines* (Little Toller Books 2017); 'Field notes, Horsmonden furnace pond' and 'Geological section' were exhibited at Tunbridge Wells Museum & Art Gallery in 2017; 'Salt works' was exhibited at St Barbe Museum & Art Gallery in 2018. 'Water spirit' and 'Cart pond' were set to music by composer Hugh Morris whose work *Three Songs from Springlines*, a commission from Ludlow English Song Weekend in 2020, was performed at Ludlow in 2021. 'Geological section' was set to music by composer Michael Bascom in 2021.

'After your procedure' won second prize in the Hippocrates Prize for Poetry and Medicine (Open section) in 2020 and was published in *The Hippocrates Prize* anthology that year. 'My son's first leather boots' was nominated for the Forward Prize for Best Single Poem 2023.

A version of 'My possible deaths' was published in my collection *Each Other* (Waterloo Press 2019). A version of 'Browsing at my desk, May 2020' was published online at *Poetry and Covid*, a project run by Anthony Caleshu, Rory Waterman and Sam Kemp. 'Offering' was aired as part of an online performance at Guildhall School of Music & Drama in 2020.

I am grateful to Rebecca Goss, Robert Hamberger, Christopher Hedley-Dent, Sarah Salway, Catherine Smith and Andrea Witzke Slot, and to the 'New Zealand Poets' (Charlotte Gann, Jeremy Page, Rachel Playforth, Peter Stewart, Janet Sutherland, Kay Syrad, Clare Whistler) for generous comradeship.

I am very glad to be able to reproduce by permission of Abner Stein, parts of 'A Litany for Survival', The Black Unicorn by Audre Lorde; W. W. Norton & Company © 1978, 1992 by Audre Lorde.

Thank you Michaela Ridgway for the cover image, and thank you Peter and Amanda Carpenter for everything else.

To Philip and Freddie – my love, and my appreciation of the distances travelled together.

for Uma and Clem

From 'A Litany for Survival' by Audre Lorde

For those of us who live at the shoreline
standing upon the constant edges of decision...

...For those of us
who were imprinted with fear
like a faint line in the center of our foreheads
learning to be afraid with our mother's milk
for by this weapon
this illusion of some safety to be found
the heavy-footed hoped to silence us
For all of us
this instant and this triumph
We were never meant to survive.

And when the sun rises we are afraid
it might not remain
when the sun sets we are afraid
it might not rise in the morning...

...when we are loved we are afraid
love will vanish
when we are alone we are afraid
love will never return
and when we speak we are afraid
our words will not be heard
nor welcomed
but when we are silent
we are still afraid.

So it is better to speak
remembering
we were never meant to survive.

Contents

Woods, Chalk, Glass

By Night

Cinder Path

By Water

Flight Path

Offering

Once there was
a bone-whistle-finger-flute
and into it
breath was played
or you could say
a mind breathed into it

and here now
hear this imagined sound
the size of a small heart
in an upturned palm
imperfect in its solitude
as we are

Woods, Chalk, Glass

A heron in a poem might seem a cliché

From my upstairs window, I saw a heron
perched on the neighbour's roof, looking rough –
like it hadn't slept in weeks. Exhausted, like me.

Then I heard my dog bark, and another
barking sound – maybe a muntjac in the lane.

I went down to look.
The heron stood barking in my garden.
It flapped off. The dog returned to bed.

I'd been back upstairs ten minutes when
the barking started again. Again, I went down –

the dog's nose at the long window,
that heron strutting across the lawn, away
from the pond. Dog two, heron nil.

The heron began to fly round and round
while I boiled the kettle, made tea.

Daylight was failing. The dog lay curled
on his rug. I was about to draw the curtains
when the heron landed by the pond,

three feet from where I stood. I froze.
It crouched by the black water and angled

its neck over the surface, staring, zooming in
on a deep carp. Fourteen times, the bird's head
plunged, came up gulping –

I saw the heron sway, extend, spear its prey
while the day's colours turned to grey on grey.

Lark walk, February

All the boundaries of the field lean in –
tangled hawthorn, lines of listing trees.

A dropped gate, off its hinges, rests
on slack wire at the join of path and track.
Tufts of caught wool flicker with the wind.

Even the uneven ground leans in,
pressing into air that presses down.

All the boundaries of the field lean in
until the field becomes the world
contained within this place of chalk
and green, while here and there, larks go up –

five, six – rising far enough to start a song,
then sink, to stay on winter ground.

Watering hole

A parched morning. Two young fallow
step out of the woods, quick with fear,

at the limits of adrenalin,
their lightning bodies snapping twigs.

I watch them pick a careful way down
to the bowl's base, muzzles lowered

to a rich dark mulch of decaying leaves,
all that's left of the drinking place –

then they're up the other side, chafing
through a rip in the fence, to a yellow field.

My mind says *dehydration, death.*
Seconds later, the rump of another fallow

soars over bracken by the old watering hole –
rear legs kicking out, scattering scent

on scorched air – all ease and vigour.
My mind says *hope, necessity.*

Did I see that third deer
or was it my wanting?

Clem, at six,

counts bees
on lavender bushes –
not bees per bush, but bees

as they hover and dance
across and under and over,
visiting, re-visiting;

she counts each bee arrive
and leave, arrive and leave,
living the blur and the buzz –

blue-scented air
and grey-green shadow, and
bees not resting

here or here
but humming,
humming.

Googling < long-tailed tit > in November

I discover a ten-hour recording
of *thhrup thhrup thhrup chi-chi-chi-chi* –
so I hit play, let it run all day as I work;

rain mists the window, tractors splash
past my house, down the narrow lane,
and for hours I'm treated to this

long-tailed recital – bringing cloudless sky,
magnolia, cherry blossom.
In my garden they don't stay ten hours

but visit in quick pink mobs, long tails
dipping – *chi-chi-chi-chi* – crowding the air
and moving on, as I've no wish to

sitting at my desk this dank November
under the magnolia in April –
wondering if song is ever temporal.

Still life with lemon

Day 3. A lemon on my glass table. Glossy and waxy even though it's unwaxed; two patches of bright-dimpled skin bounce light from window and lamp.

Day 4. Is the lemon smaller than yesterday, drier? If it rolled, it might knock precious objects. Oranges and lemons say the bells of Saint Clements.

Day 6. I learned this today: women used to cut one in half, insert the half-lemon like a diaphragm at the entrance to the cervix. Lemon juice is a natural spermicide.

Day 7. Fertility, purity, fidelity, wealth. The human heart. Lemons have properties that counter poison. Cleansing, healing. The skin is losing its gloss.

Day 8. Bowls of lemons in Dutch paintings represented power, and dominance in trading. One tiny brown pit in mine.

Day 11. Small brown pit is wider, by a millimetre or so. The lemon weighs heavy in my hand. My mouth is a reservoir of saliva.

Day 12. Two pits. It's softer. How long should I wait?

Day 16. It has a smooth flat patch, the size of my thumbnail, from relaxing on the glass. Rind yellower, darker. When I hold it to my nose, that citrus rush. Tempted to break in.

Day 17. I fetch the serrated knife, a white plate, but stop short – leave knife and plate on my side table. Tomorrow will be the day.

Day 18. Hack into the lemon – a crude bisection. Fine spray across the glass. Juice puddles on the plate. I squeeze both halves, crushing them in my hands until I'm dripping with sweet-sour sticky juice.

Day 25. Never did that. The lemon is hard and dull, pits invisible now. It sits on my glass with stones, a peacock feather, an antler, two pieces of driftwood, one small silver spoon, the skull of a fox.

Browsing at my desk, May 2020

Prohibited & Restricted Goods / Post Office
subscribe to read   La Peste   images of boats on sea
Coronavirus: Advice and updates   Redirect View
virtual festivals 2020 & 2021   artistssupportpledge – Bing

Greenpeace UK   international womens day
Authentication Service   Log in to Facebook   Love
in the Time of Cholera   Jessye Norman – Les Chemins
de l'amour (Poulenc)   grief and condolence – Bing

How to Grow Your Own Tomatoes, 1: Starting Seeds…
French Revolution key dates   Sourdough for beginners
Pandemic being used as cover for no-deal Brexit
Citrus Salmon – Loriana Shea Cooks   apocalypse – Bing

Reasons For Fig Tree Not Fruiting   a man's reunion
with his donkey after quarantine…   oil price May 2020
How to Grow Your Own Tomatoes, 2: Transplanting…
Sign In – Zoom   not working   what do jays eat – Bing

5 Best Pulse Oximeters Reviews 2020   join conversation
cheesy puff pastry onion tart   Maxi Dresses – Page 2
origin and meaning of quiet   Microsoft Teams – error
distance from durham to barnard castle – Bing

Sign In – Twitter   Share petition – Dominic Cummings
must be sacked…   Negative thinking linked
to Alzheimers – bioreport   The Stage – News
Great Spotted Woodpecker   total excess deaths – Bing

How to Grow Your Own Tomatoes, 3: Staking, Training…
Sign In – Zoom   Log in to Facebook   Cannot Open Page
How to Grow Your Own Tomatoes, 4: Disease
Prevention…   Track and Trace Your Large Parcel

In Markstakes Wood

whichever track you take
        you will always be lost

two white squirrels
        live in the holly grove

the oak by the pond
        split in October's storm

and no-one knows
        where the branches point

rain has muted the sky
        it can tell you nothing

beyond the gate

in memory of Sarah Everard
and all the others

scots pine and resin-scented air
    out here
giant oak   next to the path
    we are walking

sycamore   in sun   in shade
holly crowding ragged elder

sweet chestnut   spruce fir   douglas fir
    with us
field maple   half-uprooted beech
    out here   walking

sorbus domestica   the service tree
and elm   rare elm

blackthorn   black with sloes
    with us   out here
hawthorn   hazel   leaning ash
    and we are walking

ivy   juniper   cherry   poplar
copper beech and twisted willow

so many hornbeam   so many birch
    out here
stripped leafless by fine sleet
    as we are   walking

ranks of cypress   sapling larch
branches creaking high above

wild plum and wild pear
      we are   we are
scarred   black-leafed   still with fruit
      walking   walking

By Night

At WH Smith, Brighton Station

I choose a black Europa notebook, the last packet
of HB pencils, a sharpener and latex-free eraser
because I must record that here, this evening,
I'm a stranger to my past.

Did I ever live in Lewes and rattle over the Downs,
toss pebbles into waves on Kemp Town beach
and queue for late-night chips? Have I
been here hundreds of times?

The person at the till is young, and friendly
in that only-in-Brighton way. *Will you
be using the pencils to sketch in the book?*
I nod, shake my head, nod again –

by now even I'm confused. *I'm a writer.
But I came all this way without notebook or pencils.*
A patient smile. *I hope you and your muse
have a beautiful night.*

The pools at Glyndebourne

When I leave the garden, the first lake,
step through the gate into a wilderness
of bright peninsulas and inlets
dense with tree limbs slung or broken

when crows gather over the shining field
when a heron or the ghost of a heron
stands at the water's edge and I'm not sure
what I've seen, not sure of anything

when greylag geese fetch dusk
or the moorhen quits her bronze nest
at the heart of a great wide sea, I know
a dream has surfaced, pulled me in.

★

The Bourne drops
through a tight cut
in the chalky wall – stirs
and swells this pond
whose banks are thick
with acid nettles, moss,
the whitened roots
of ash and elder –
and stays a short while
before stealing on
across wet fields
to join Glynde Reach,
the Sussex Ouse.

★

House and lawns are quite invisible
         from here, the last pool,
with its cubicles of unclipped yew.

The stream eases over weed
         and fallen branches,
translates the image of a flat grey sky
         to molten silver
and this spring morning

to an August night decades ago
         when swimmers
left their clothes
         under the stars
and slipped into velvet water.

Once my home

A loud splinter-crack as hinges spring free of the frame and the front door falls away from me. I step inside, onto years of gnarled, twisted rootwork – long root fingers becoming longer before my eyes, reaching towards the ancient core of the house, away from light angling through windows.

I clamber over fibrous root systems, rough and smooth. Roots seek darkness; they make what they seek. The old house has become a spongy bed of compost. A few seedlings erupt from this friable soil – twigs with leaf buds at their tips. Lying down, my ear to one of the fattest roots, I know a pale, whispered calm, like distant low singing formed of vowel sounds.

The stairwell is a tangle of feeder roots around familiar painted banisters. I know every scrape and scratch. Now I climb up, up, to find what has sent roots down. The smooth trunk of a giant beech tree rises into branches, twigs, silky leaves. At the top – everything is space, air.

Using Greenwood's Large-Scale Map of the County of Suffolk (1825) to find my friend's house

Slow through rain and murk – down School Lane,
past the gate to Captain's Wood,
left on Ferry Road, left again by Red House Farm
and then a mile of Roman road and sandy track –

back two hundred years along dotted lines
between black ditches, over wooden bridges
to the edge of the eastern reaches –

fields dissolve, the settle of shingle almost audible;
somewhere close, an invisible river lags
its silty way through marsh and curlew country.

He calls it his lonely house –
this place at the land's precarious rim.
I hear him slide the bolt of the old oak door,
see him standing tall in a shutter of light.

Portent

It was already late; darkness close.
We set off with the dog
and a sense of imminence.

Stripes of light scarred the horizon –
we counted booms and seconds,
tried to work out how far we might get.

My bare hand gripped your bare hand.
The dog pressed between us.
Birches swayed and creaked, wet leaves

reeked of fear. Our phones
needled the dark; we stumbled
on roots. Branches dropped around us.

When the sky glowed orange and purple
we knew it was time –
I turned for home and you followed.

Hard hat

I couldn't see the nurses for dust, and the ceiling
was hanging down in the room they said was mine;
now and then a man in hi-vis overalls walked past
with clanking tool belt and grin. Screech and rip
of metal cutters, bangs, clatters, thumps as walls
collapsed. After an hour they brought a hard hat –
awkward to wear lying on my back but it gave me
some illusion of protection. Strip lights flickered
and flashed, windows rattled, the whole building
shook. A crane swung over and I was lifted gently
into a sling, raised through a night sky full of stars,
fireworks, smoke, until I could see all of London
and my newborn son, taking his first dusty breath
as they strapped a miniature helmet onto his head.

Rising in the night, in summer

Seven hours my son has been driving us
through lush deep grass. Although it's dark
I'm aware of an edge. I'm okay because I'm
in the passenger seat – but in fact I'm not
okay because I'm stiff with fear; my son is
in the driver's seat, nearest the sixty-degree
slope. He's staring resolutely ahead and
the car bounces and swerves through mist
above a chalky combe. The edge goes on
and on. And I keep saying: *Slower! Please
be careful, we could go over.* My son has
a soothing voice: *Mum, I'm in charge, we'll
be all right, I promise, but I must drive us
to where we're going. The bats are there.*

My son's first leather boots

It's not the memories they evoke –
there are plenty, but I won't list them here,
they might escape. It's not the number 25

stamped on the instep next to a little box
that says Start-rite, nor the crusts of mud
stuck in the treads twenty-four years.

It's not scuffed toes, heels worn down
in one particular place. Not deep creases
at the ankles where brown polish lingers.

Even if I cherish details, it's not those.
It's this: I have to close my door, sit
quietly and alone with love and mystery.

St Lucy's Day, 4.15 pm

A blackbird in the cherry tree
gathers and stitches quiet
into a song for this terse day.

Cold air bristles with sudden dark.
Two robins serenade the street lamp
while children settle in luminous rooms.

She walks into her garden
under invisible stars, to find
and rake and heap late-fallen leaves –

bleached oak and silver birch bark
lighting her path through night
into tomorrow, next year.

Last thing

for Flint (Kennel Club name: Blandings Inspired by Grace)

First I stroke his silky head
then squeeze paste,
gather cheek and lip,
draw them back
with index finger and thumb.

He starts to turn away
but I know he trusts
because as soon as I
run bristles along gums
his head rests heavy in my hand,
his eyes stay with mine.

I smooth the blanket,
rinse the brush.
His ears twitch
under spray from the tap.

When I flick off the light
and speak into darkness,
Goodnight, darling one,
I'm wondering how
I lifted him from the litter,
held him to my chest
as his mother stared.

Cinder Path

Salting

all through the long wet spring
the river   turns away
into bracken   sodden peat
sunlight skimming the surface

moss   ferns   honeysuckle
froth collecting by roots
leaves   spun in the churn

no warning was given
that there would be
so much blood

that it would ooze
day after day
from a wounded core

and when the bleeding ceased
I said nothing
I was mute

years later I can say
my body bled
I bled

silt where the river narrows
water sings over acorns   stones
a frayed bough drifts   and twists

is it the same water?
forest green
dimpled by water boatmen

river funnels   into a basket of twigs

no warning was given either
about the milk

nothing was said
and when the milk came
I said nothing

but years later I tell myself
my body made milk

                water plays   snatches leaves
                        each one sinks deep
                      rises again   spinning
      oak   beech   hornbeam   holly   birch

no way to know
when tears would come
when they would not

no way to know
some would compose
a dead sea inside

years later I can say
the sea has dried
to a salting of words

                moss   ferns   honeysuckle
                  froth collecting by roots
            leaves   spun in the churn
                          listen

home now from that place
home   with this bright blood
I will be mother to my first son

but not to you   my second
there must be a future   there is
a future tense

things   will   be
I lie in bed   trying to think
our lives will be   yours will not

will there be love? will there be
love enough
without a future?

after blood and milk
will there be rest and sleep?
I hope   I hope

I am home
without my second son
no one to imagine

                    a beech leans out
            gathering rippled shade

        the flow is dammed by logs

        diamond-patterned water
                    scooping mud

you are my midlife dream
you are   what I want you to be
mauve-pink lips   skin pale with vernix

you will be loved   you
will be everything
so late late did we candle you into being

I remember your weight inside me
hours waiting for that call
those words   *foetal*

abnormalities
I know nothing   what should I know?
I am this and that   I am stone

you are   in my head
in my uterus   you lazy lazarus of babies
I will always love you

you are my rage   my comfort
enough enough
beloved child   how I want you

cold table where I sit
hours of trance   unable to feel
light leaning in a garden

I stay until darkness
until I am sure   only of dark
sitting at the kitchen table

you in my belly   knowing
unknowing   knowing
what I can do   will do   cannot undo

how I can or cannot   let you be
I am   I am not   you are
I weigh my life in yours through years

my yes I must and no I cannot
restless dreaming
restless love   you are flight

and capture   meeting this deep breath
in me   such death in me
again again again again

                                silt where the river narrows

                                water sings over stones
                                hurries from this pool
                                through gravel shallows
                                to the next

                                is it the same water?
                                forest green
                                dimpled by water boatmen

                                a place before the first place
                                where the river turns away
                                into bracken   sodden peat
                                and sunlight skims the surface

After your procedure

go straight home   it will take a while
you will bleed   slowly heavily
you may have cramps   in circles
do not walk or drive   on your own
wear loose clothing   cry when you can
hold a hot water bottle to your lower abdomen   be aware of a space inside

do not shower without someone nearby   now & then you might fall
you might feel light-headed   you might always feel light-headed

the speed of your recovery   the extent of your recovery
will depend on your procedure   will depend on your grief
you should wait several weeks   that cannot be measured
before resuming physical work or sport   try to accept
you will soon be fit again   you will never be the same

you might feel relieved or sad   think of a crater
or (more often) a mix of emotions   how quick (slow) the healing
take plenty of water   for the place you will become

resist strenuous activity & if poppies & nettles take root
spend time with friends   moths & bees will return

On this day

the forest floor is soft and damp
oak bark bronzed by sun

always on this day
the leaf litter under my feet
seems impossibly deep
sky too thin
alive with birds I cannot hear
                    or see

the forest bears its broken trees
unpicks its dead

always on this day
year after year
I walk my path
remembering I walk my path
                    remembering

The words

Gravid   Bun in the oven   Stung by a serpent
In the pudding club   Eating for two

       Deliberate miscarriage

Tin roof rusted   Knocked up   With child
Pea in the pod   Bat in the cave   Caught the baby flu

       Embryoctony   Abortion

Preggers   Keith Cheggars   Carrying a uterine parasite
Wearing the bustle wrong   In the family way   In a fix

       Misbirth   Termination

The rabbit died   Alien belly   In pig   Up the duff
Up the spout   Up the pole   Up the stick

       Feticide

What do we know?

she suffers from night terrors
she's a single mother
she loves her husband
she's 13   she's 49   she's 28
her sister lives too far away
she feels completely alone
she already has three children
she has no children
she looks after her mother   father   uncle
she's exhausted
her daughter's in prison
her partner's in prison
she feels as though she's in prison
she's depressed
she was raped by her neighbour
boyfriend   brother
she takes pride in working hard
she can't afford childcare
she's exhausted
she's always wanted this baby
she never wanted this baby
she can't look after a baby
she only gets a few hours sleep each night
she's addicted to prescription painkillers
she's on a waiting list
for rehab   for therapy
she's woman not god
she's exhausted
she's working out how to be the best mother
this might be her only way to be the best mother

By Water

Three poems about fog

That morning, we left the house in fog,
drove to the airport through fog.

Foggy when we parked, checked in,
climbed the steps to the plane.

Only a short flight in and out of cloud
and the place we landed flat and thick

with fog. On the train: grey glass, grey air,
nothing to drink but water vapour.

For a week I never saw the far bank
of the river, your hand reaching for mine.

We were close but kept losing each other.
Back home, fog rolled off the sea –

now it swirls around the sofa, the fridge,
our kitchen table with its pile of keys.

★

Before, I'd only known
fog over ice

and known the ice was thin
and heard it crack.

Look out, thin ice! I'd tell myself.
Step back. Run!

★

But I stayed with you
and ice and fog.

In the well-house, December

I want to drop into the well's throat –
           I want to be
two hundred feet down
where water vibrates

but I stand at this open mouth –
        shaking with cold,
pouring water – I need
to hear water on water.

Book of water

This volume's heavy, difficult to hold: the mossy
cover oozes green, springs rise across two pages
of Acknowledgements. Here's the Introduction:
mud. Chapter One: a story bubbles along the spine,
trickles into print, disappears. Two: clouds mass
above a coronal of ancient trees, rain meets
gravity's reach, down, down to the lower margin.
In Chapter Three paper goes to pulp. Four: water
governs earth and sky. Elm trees sway on tides
of seed. Oaks withstand the longest storm.
What book is this where water
will not stay but runs, forgets? Afterword, Index,
Colophon: a flood has swept away the final pages.

Dewpond

I am a dent in the ancient Downs –
shallow crater, unhealed wound. I am lens,
bright coin on the dip slope's tongue.

I am the shock of water
filling the hollow left by the hoof.
I am found at the heart of a midnight storm,

in the pause after the snow's rough song.
Sink to your knees in my summer dew,
autumn rain and sleet.

Held by chalk-light
between sky and hill, I mirror the dark
night after night. I am thought

by earth and air, gorse and hawthorn.
Under the sun, I shrink
To a sliver of platinum. I am gone.

Cart pond

Low sky. Low mist. Oak leaves curl
the surface of the pond. This pool
is dark green, old. Carts once
stopped here on summer afternoons –

tall nettles, light playing on water,
oxen and horses drinking at the pond's
perimeter as men dragged
the cart frames in deep and deeper

to slake the wood of iron-tyred wheels.
At dusk, the men waded back in,
hauled out the carts – everything
fitting again, for now.

Summer, cart wheels, clear water.
All known, forgotten. Half-submerged.
Like those men rolling the carts down
and into the pool's heart.

Geological section

In the fine-grained sand of the faulted valley
the chalybeate spring keeps rising
through layers of mottled clay

with seams of ironstone (siderite or chalybite)
weathering to heavy soil, starved of lime,
oozing rusty ferrous water.

Rain falls on this ground,
seeps downdip, gathering in the hollow
floored by Wadhurst Clay. The spring rises

where the water table meets the surface

floored by Wadhurst Clay. The spring rises,
seeps downdip, gathering in the hollow.
Rain falls on this ground

oozing rusty ferrous water,
weathering to heavy soil starved of lime
with seams of ironstone (siderite or chalybite).

Through layers of mottled clay
the chalybeate spring keeps rising
in the fine-grained sand of the faulted valley.

salt works

after Mr St Barbe's notebook

when the sea boils
tide is admitted

from high to low
thin grey brine

in level partitions
until the last hour

then fires glow
crusting the salt

& the men know
when boiling brine

a pan yields 12 bushels
every 12 hours

& the men go on
stoking the fires

year after year
boiling brine

6 days & 6 nights
flowing fast

into feeding ponds
passing in troughs

of sun & wind
when coal is burned

to simmer the brine
in iron pans

18 bushels of coal
make 2 tons of salt

of well drained salt
of wind & tide

forever employed
come rain or shine

day & night
as the sea boils

Field notes, Horsmonden furnace pond

There be furnaces on every side, and a huge deal of wood is yearly burnt;
to which purpose diverse brooks in many places are brought to run in one
channel, and sundry meadows turned into pools and waters, that they might
be of power sufficient to drive hammer mills, which beating upon the iron,
resound over the places adjoining.
William Camden, *Britannia* (1607)

drizzle brings swallows
fieldfares   chiffchaffs   blackcaps
great crested grebes

200 furnace workers
+ miners woodcutters charcoal-burners

luggers of timber and ore to the furnace
pig iron from furnace to forge

three mandarin drakes fly in
cormorants   red-legged partridge
a charm of goldfinch

7 tons of shot + 6 cast-iron minions
for the pinnace Primrose

130 cast-iron sakers
90 culverins for the Netherlands

two buzzards circling
nuthatch   moorhen   cuckoo
black-backed gulls glide over

300 demi-culverins + 200 sakers
for the King (owing £16,000)

20 sakers for the St Claude
5 tons of shot (culverin to small falcon)

                              sparrowhawk displaying
                           lesser whitethroat singing
            marsh tits   sand martins   waxwings

cross-barred and double cross-barred shot
coupled flat shot – base and burr

bronze guns for navy vessels
Leopard, Unicorn, Swallow

                         two sandpipers drop from the gloom
                           greater spotted woodpeckers
                                         drumming

Water spirit

Jack squats
      by the weed-green pool
watching water
                tumble
    swirl and ditch
chasing
      into the drown-dark –
endless flow work

all sap-skin
     Jack sinks
            into writhing wetblack –

head dipping under
             and up
the fierce joy-ache
     of his frozen skull
and the red iron tang

making him
     flip-kick
   spit-laugh
shiver-grin

windhints trick-track
     air teases water
           teases Jack
resting in the deep
inkdark under

          windcricked
Jack slow-turns
lift-drifting
                    quicker now
          swells and churns
black stroke blue
      mudspins
                    curls
reaches up
          bending into sliplight

slick-backed
all awake Jack
          breaks through

and surface-dances

trembling with ripple work

Lecanomancy

I lower plates into suds,
study ripples and bubbles –
how they swell and dance.

You take everything
I hand you, and dry it.
We do this in silence.

When it's finished
we kiss, look through
the window over the sink

and agree this water
is unlikely
to reveal the future;

winter-growing grass
might tell us more.

Flight Path

Return to Lago Maggiore, March 2022

masks will drop from above
blue and white violets for healing
emergency lighting to guide you

cover your nose and mouth
wood anemone has a musky scent
put on your own before helping others

pay attention to illuminated signs
spiked rampion can be eaten raw
you may need to remove your shoes

lesser periwinkle or fiore di morte
binds the soil against erosion
give yourself plenty of time

citrus medica produces
clusters of pink-white flowers
the nearest exit could be behind you

Of seasons

we discern so little, and often
what we think we understand
is hearsay, expectation –

      how early frosts will shock
      in late October,
      snowdrops illuminate February.

What can we ever know of time's
disjunctions? At any hour
of any day, anything can happen.

Robert, one of my great-uncles,
poisoned himself at a Wiltshire vicarage,
an autumn night in 1916, aged 32.

A year later, in Toronto,
his brother Alan used a gun.
He was 30.

Their sister, my grandmother,
lived until she died, aged 91,
not knowing who she was.

      I've heard blackbirds sing loudest
      on dark March mornings
      when dawn is still a rumour.

T-Junction

I'm nineteen, passed my test a year ago –
     I'm turning right in broad daylight,
indicating as I should and looking carefully
     right / left – right / left – right again,
inching forward (but distracted by hunger
     and thoughts of that beautiful long-
haired boy I met last night) when a life-size
     black-leather human puppet arcs
over my bonnet. I'm transfixed by this figure
     calculating a geometry as it goes;

I've not yet seen the shiny new Norton
     motorbike – grounded now.
As far as I'm aware, this performer is here
     to show me acts of derring-do.
Halfway over, the puppet stalls for a while –
     pinned to a wispy cloud, sun
squinting around one shoulder so that
     the helmet acquires a full halo.

In a minute, I'll hear grinding brakes,
     the shriek and crunch of metal –
I'll feel the tilt and lurch, sudden stop, springs
     sprung. My chest will thump, my guts
twist and heave. But for now, all is peaceful –
     that puppet hanging in my vision
until I turn towards a sharp tap-tapping
     at my window. I wind it down.
The scuffed angel stands there, quite upright,
     and from a terrible hollow silence
asks: *Why the hell did you do that?*
     And I have no words.

A14

shifting left to right   slow lane middle lane
back to slow lane   indicator tick-tick-tick
indicator off   rearview articulated truck
coming up fast on inside   grey van slides
right   slides left again   silver sun glaring
off wet tarmac   pink motorhome sashays
strays speeds up in slow lane middle lane
sliproad traffic filters in   check wing mirror
check rearview mirror   check speed check
time   check fuel gauge going down   low-
loader stacked with scaffold planks   bumps
rattles   clangs in and out over dotted lines
check rearview check wing   think pull out
into fast lane   high lit-up digital sign   con-
gestion ahead   quick tuck back in behind
low-loader   stay dead centre middle lane
check speed spray-wipe screen   soaked
scaffold boards   wagging   must overtake
think indicate check rearview mirror   foot
down   soundless single slow-motion board
slips its rope tilts   wobbles   bounces free
drifts and floats   will land   somewhere
think brake quick   no no accelerate think
swerve think quicker think foot   down foot
down think foot down   grip wheel   think

It was always my head

or parts of my head, that had problems:
one sinus missing, all the others sized
for a small child, which was okay at first
but I grew and my sinuses didn't;
my eyes (crossed, wandering, or both)
were subject to surgery – once, twice –
then spectacles with prisms, all the time;

my skull ached if I moved, bent over –
one day it was so bad I couldn't turn
my head, couldn't see through the lights:
the doctor came and made me try to
bow as though you're praying – but this
was impossible, it hurt far too much.
No prayers that day. The doctor phoned

for an ambulance; I was rolled in grey felt,
stretchered by two faceless men down
the bright staircase: *keep your eyes shut*
bump bump bump – out in the cold
a long sliding action, clunk, and now
strapped in with leather belts, doors
slamming, engine churning. Sometimes

I'm still in that rush – stirred by pain,
siren, pulsing blue – and I curse my head
until I think of those nurses, how they
laid me out, quickly prepared my spine
for their needle, taking care to explain
the head is connected to everything:
fingers, toes, heart, whole body, life.

Burning

I've tasted it before, in this boy's mouth.
He says, Come on! Why not try *one*.
Okay I'm ready, I tell him. So he
lights up, leans across and slips the fag

between my lip-glossed lips. A bonfire!
But I suck it, suck like it's giving me
life – wet Players filter, halting drag

of bitter smoke. Oh yes, I'm trying.
He teaches me how to inhale, hold on,
then exhale politely over my shoulder.

I still have the Instamatic snap he took
at The Anchor on our last date – me
in a black dress, blowing smoke rings,
fairground goldfish trapped in a bowl.

Eighteen years and fifty thousand fags
later, just two months married, in love
with my love in a tiny top-floor flat,
and he falls ill for Christmas – can't

lift his head to smoke. My chance
finally to go cold turkey. By the time
he's back on his feet, we've both quit.

I must have last lit up on Boxing Day
that year. I can't now recall the brand,
how it tasted. Did I blow smoke rings?

I've no snap to tell me that, or what
I was wearing. My closing fag went un-
noted. One of those endings that only
afterwards turns out to be an ending.

Late fig

mid-
winter
gift
hangs
in thin air

after a fig-summer
when I learned to gorge
figs and goat's cheese and honey
with bread rich as Christmas pudding
long summer of squeezing lemon moons
over fine fig-slices to make fig-flesh bleed then
feasting on it   lemon-reddened   after that I fear
disappointment   but this single fig-surpassing fig
has fully perfect unsplit satin fig-skin   purple-green
darkly tender   I reach up and the gift gives slightly to
my carefully cultivated fig-touch   does not resist a fig-
knife cutting it against white porcelain   this precious
late fruit proves super fig-charged with intricate
red-pink and butter-coloured ravelled riches
and there at its centre a mysterious
shady hollow   the very heart
of figness

I'm writing

because I must give thanks
for hours   minutes   weeks
because this morning I woke
early   in the dark   and knew
a moment's bleak despair
your body not with mine

because I didn't move
or reach for you   and tried
to look   but couldn't see
because I listened   for breath
a hand whispering the sheet
the slight shift of your head

because now I understand
a different kind of arrival
into time   woken by your
not being here   and because
one day   it will be   just this
if you go first and I am left

Self-portrait as boundary oak

A few of us still mark the forest's edge
though some are dead or tilting.

I'm fonder of bones than I was, proud
of creviced bark, circles of growth, years

enclosing heartwood. Each storm
sways me further out over a sandy field

or in towards crowded and earthy places;
it's late – I breathe, and I listen to breath.

Shadows pencil my skin this cold afternoon
before the green blooding of spring.

My possible deaths

When I feel ready, I go down
and open the front door
to see more than forty of them
standing, chatting.

All day I wonder
how many will still be there
by nightfall, and I spend time
finding things for their comfort –

I want to make them comfortable.
I arrange objects on the grass
close to the house:
cushions, books, magazines,

red and green apples,
cheese and bread.
They take what they want
then move away into the trees.

I watch from an upper window;
by evening, almost all of them
are gone. Just three return
the next day and the next,

week after week after week,
helping themselves to my offerings –
I try to think of them
as companions, friends.

Flowers,

lavished on me night after night
while I lie on my back
on warm soft ground
in the dark.

I know them by their scent,
the gentle touch
of stem and leaf and petal:
lilies of the valley,
wood anemones,
tight buds of clematis montana,
immaculate star magnolia;

each night I close my eyes
and imagine a line of people
bringing flowers
to cover my body.

Wake

All of a sudden in an Irish place,
at the house I've just moved into
in a village I barely know and yet
I've been here my entire life;

chaotic, fun, with everyone I love
on a sloping lawn gorging oranges,
chocolate cake, grapes and brie,
playing with all the dogs I ever had,
filling up long glasses until

Veuve Cliquot spills everywhere
and raucous laughter spreads
when a shower of summer rain
bursts from clear skies and sinks
all the feet in mud, and someone
climbs on a chair, claps their hands:

*It might not seem completely obvious
but this is exactly what she would
have liked – so dig in, help yourselves
to plenty. And godspeed.*

Crossing the Styx in the Quiet Carriage

This was a big mistake. The Quiet Carriage isn't quiet,
it shudders with envy, lust, neurosis, fatigue, regret –
rendered more palpable by the desire for peace.
Those of us who reserve these quiet seats
are super-sensitive. Our skins are thinner.

A woman with a condescending voice insists, *Welcome
aboard this* Great *British Railway Service*, her words
accompanied by a sonic rainbow of nose-blowings,
slurps, sneezes, whispers, foot-shufflings,
gut-rumblings, crackling KitKat wrappers.

WhatsApp alerts vie with announcements: *Please
leave all your belongings behind. We're approaching our final
destination, where this life terminates. Take care stepping down.*
My time here will soon be done; I'll walk
into authentic silence, uninterruptible air.

Epitaph

was never good at finding root or base
not gifted at things mathematical

could only be present
in this day
in mind   heart   body
seldom wanting to find a way out

skilled at moving towards the light
at discovering blue and green

could marvel   could sing
was alive
to hunger and thirst
craved the sting of salt water on skin

Notes on poems

Browsing at my desk, May 2020 (p 12)

This found poem, written from my browsing history in spring and summer 2020, aims to project some of the strangeness and fearfulness of the lockdown mind, teased by the comforts and frustrations of online existence.

After your procedure (p 38)

The text in italics on the left side of the poem was found on a US website offering advice for recovery following surgical termination of pregnancy.

The words (p 40)

A found poem that brings together slang synonyms for pregnancy with synonyms for pregnancy termination.

Geological section (p 50)

Draw an imaginary line from Wellington Rocks at 410 ft above sea level (Lower Tunbridge Wells Sandstone over Wadhurst Clay) to Rumbers Hill at 489 ft above sea level (Ashdown Sand). The spring rises almost exactly halfway along this line.

salt works (p 51)

The marshes at Lymington in Hampshire were at the centre of an important area of salt production for more than seven hundred years, until rising salt taxes and the cost of transporting vast quantities of coal over long distances tipped the industry into decline in the mid-19th century. Mr Charles St Barbe (after whom the St Barbe Museum & Art Gallery in Lymington is named) kept detailed notebooks about salt production in his extensive salterns.

Field notes, Horsmonden furnace pond (p 52)

Here is a glossary of some terms used in this account of Wealden iron production in the seventeenth century.

Culverin: Long-range heavy cannon. Its name derives from coluber, the Latin word for serpent.

Demi-culverin: This cannon was larger than a saker but smaller than a regular culverin. The barrel was about 11 ft long. Used in sieges for wall and building demolition.

Saker: Medium cannon, slightly smaller than a demi-culverin. Named after the saker falcon. The barrel was 9½ ft long.

Minion: Smaller cannon often used on ships. The Pilgrim Fathers took a minion on the Mayflower.

Small falcon: Light cannon with a barrel about 4 ft long.

Pinnace: Boat propelled by oars or sails, carried aboard a merchant or war vessel to ferry water, provisions and armed sailors for boarding expeditions.

Lecanomancy (p 56)
Divination by inspection of water in a basin.